Sit & Solve

BASEBALL TRIVIA

**DOM FORKER &
WAYNE STEWART**

Sterling Publishing Co., Inc.
New York

Edited by Claire Bazinet

4 6 8 10 9 7 5 3

Published by Sterling Publishing Co., Inc.
387 Park Avenue South, New York, NY 10016
Copyright © 2005 by Dom Forker and Wayne Stewart
Material in this book excerpted from
Test Your Baseball IQ © 1993 by Dom Forker
and *Baseball Bafflers* © 1999 by Wayne Stewart
Distributed in Canada by Sterling Publishing
⅝ Canadian Manda Group, 165 Dufferin Street
Toronto, Ontario, Canada M6K 3H6
Distributed in Great Britain by Chrysalis Books Group PLC
The Chrysalis Building, Bramley Road, London W10 6SP, England
Distributed in Australia by Capricorn Link (Australia) Pty. Ltd.
P.O. Box 704, Windsor, NSW 2756, Australia

Sterling ISBN 1-4027-2146-3
For information about custom editions, special sales, premium and
corporate purchases, please contact Sterling Special Sales
Department at 800-805-5489 or specialsales@sterlingpub.com

CONTENTS

FOREWORD

This book is perfect for the "spectating player" who loves the history, the strategy, and the unpredictability of baseball. It will inform, entertain, intrigue, and test your knowledge of the sport—and the rule book— from all positions. Match-up quips by players and managers also bring baseball's colorful characters to vivid life. So let's "Play ball!"

BATTING

Sharing an At-Bat

Casey Stengel is playing with his batting order and alternating Phil Rizzuto and Billy Martin in the number-one and number-eight spots. On Friday, he had Martin batting first and Rizzuto eighth. On Saturday, Martin steps into the batter's box to begin the game at Briggs Stadium in Detroit. Tiger pitcher Hal Newhouser runs a count of no balls and two strikes on Martin before Rizzuto realizes he is the named lead-off batter for the Yankees for this game. The "Scooter" rushes up and takes Martin's place in the batter's box. On Newhouser's next pitch Rizzuto swings and misses.

Is anyone called out for batting out of order here? Who is charged with the strikeout?

Answer on page 14.

4

Double Penalty

An Oakland A's batter is at the plate in the top half of the seventh inning with two out, a three-two count, and the bases loaded. Just as the Mariner pitcher is about to go into his wind-up, the batter steps out of the box and asks the umpire for time-out. The arbiter doesn't give it to him! The pitcher pitches. Scott Bradley, the Seattle catcher, has to jump to prevent the pitch from sailing for a wild pitch. What's the call?

Answer on page 14.

5

Leaning over the Plate

Minnie Minoso of the White Sox liked to lean over the plate. (As a result he led the major leagues in career hit-by-pitches until Don Baylor broke his record.) One day in 1955, leaning over the plate, he was hit with a three-two pitch in the strike zone by Whitey Ford of the Yankees. Did the umpire give Minoso a hit-by-pitch award or a walk?

Answer on page 15.

The Sultan's Bat

The Official Baseball Rules specifies that no bat can be longer than 42 inches or more than 2¾ inches in diameter. Rule 1.10 [a]. Does it also limit the weight of the bat?

Answer on page 15–16

The Way the Ball Bounces

6

On August 22, 1992, with no runners on base in a scoreless tie, Charlie Hayes of the Yankees, hit a pitch by Chuck Finley of the Angels high and far down the left-field line at Yankee Stadium. The ball hit the wire netting extending along the side of the foul pole and rebounded to left fielder Luis Polonia in fair territory. Did the third-base umpire rule the hit a foul ball, a home run, a double, or a ball still in play?

Answer on page 16–17.

Swinging
Third Strike

One of the most famous plays in baseball history took place in the bottom of the ninth inning of Game Three of the 1941 World Series.

The Brooklyn Dodgers, down to the Yankees two games to one, were leading, 4-3, with two out and no one on base. Tommy Henrich was the batter for New York; Hugh Casey was the pitcher for Brooklyn. The count ran to three-and-two on Henrich. Then Casey broke off a hard curve—some said it was a spitter—and Henrich swung and missed.

The game would have been over then, but the ball got away from catcher Mickey Owen and rolled back to the screen as Henrich ran safely to first base.

Then the roof fell in on Brooklyn. Joe DiMaggio singled and Charlie Keller doubled two runs home. After Bill Dickey walked, Joe Gordon doubled two more runs across the plate.

The Yankees won the game, 7-4.

7

When Henrich had swung and missed, it had seemed for a moment that Brooklyn had tied the Series at two games apiece. Instead, the Yankees ended up with a commanding three-games-to-one lead. The next day the Yankees won again, 3-1, and wrapped up a Series they very well could have lost. In retrospect, though, wasn't Henrich's swinging strike the third out of the inning and the final out of the game?

Answer on page 17.

A "Heads-Up" Play

A batter's long fly ball bounces off the center-field fence, strikes the outfielder on the head, and bounces into the stands. The umpire awards the batter a ground-rule double. Is the ruling a good one?

Answer on page 18.

The
Ground-Rule Triple

There are many ways for a batter to hit a ground-rule double.
He can: 1) hit a ball in fair territory that bounces into the stands,
2) hit a ball that a fan touches in leaning over the rail, 3) hit a ball that
deflects off any base into the stands, or 4) hit a ball which deflects off a
fielder's glove, in fair territory, and bounces into the stands in foul territory.
But is there any way a batter can hit a ground-rule triple?

Answer on page 18–19.

9

Distracting the Batter

With Wade Boggs of the Red Sox at the plate, the Twins' second baseman
positions himself directly behind the second base bag and jumps up and
down, waving his arms, in an attempt to distract the Boston third
baseman's focus. Is this legal?

Answer on page 19.

Pine-Tar Play

Thurman Munson of the Yankees has just driven home a run in a 1975 game against the Twins. But the Twins' manager, claiming that Munson has too much pine tar on his bat, appeals the play. (The rules permit up to 18 inches of pine tar from the handle to the barrel.) Upon examination, the umpires find that the pine tar significantly exceeds the maximum limit. What do the umpires do?

Answer on page 20.

10

Pine-Tar Reprise

Some time after Munson's pine-tar incident, there was the more famous 1983 one at Yankee Stadium.

The Royals were trailing the Yankees, 3-2, in the top of the ninth. With two out, and no one on base, U.L. Washington singled off reliever Goose Gossage, and George Brett followed with an upper-deck homer that gave the Royals a 4-3 lead. The Yankees filed an appeal, which the umpires upheld, based on the amount of pine tar on Brett's bat. Brett was called out for using an illegal bat. So New York left the field with an apparent 3-2 victory. But the Royals protested to the American League president, Lee McPhail. Did McPhail uphold the protest?

Answer on page 21.

Chasing a Pitch

11

A well-known slugger is batting against a pitcher who hasn't been having all that much success against him recently. The hurler decides to throw a floater. The pitch is too tempting for the batter to let go, so he runs up on the ball and, with his front foot out of the batter's box, hits the pitch for a home run. Is it a legal one?

Answer on page 21–22.

Taking One
for the Team

Don Baylor was the career champ at getting hit by pitchers. But several times during his career he was hit by a pitch and not awarded first base. In which situations may a batter be hit by a pitch and not be awarded first base?

Answer on page 22.

12

Fist Ball

The Twins batter has a count of two balls and two strikes when he swings and misses a Dave Stewart fastball. But the ball hits the batter's fist and bounces into foul territory down the first-base line. Catcher Terry Steinbach of the A's pounces on the ball and throws it to first baseman Mark McGwire, who steps on the base. Did the A's have to make the above play?

Answer on page 22.

Is Sacrifice
an At-Bat?

Ken Griffey of the host Mariners is on third base with no out in a 3-3 game with the Oakland A's. Kevin Mitchell, the Mariners batter, hits a long fly ball that center fielder Willie Wilson catches near the fence in left-center. Griffey scores on the play.

Does Mitchell get an RBI, exempting him from an at-bat?

Answer on page 23.

13

BASEBALL QUOTABLE

After hitting four homers in a game to tie the single-game record, power hitter Bob Horner said quite correctly, "I had a good week today."

BATTING ANSWERS

Sharing an At-Bat

Rizzuto, as the proper batter, gets charged with the strikeout. No one is called out for batting out of order. The proper batter may take his place in the batter's box at any time before the improper batter becomes a runner or is put out, and any balls and strikes shall be counted in the proper batter's time at bat. Rule 6.07 [a].

Double Penalty

The pitch, though wild, is called an automatic strike, the batter is out, and the inning is over. The umpire doesn't *have* to give the batter time-out if he feels that it was requested too late or for the wrong reason. It is the batter's responsibility to know whether the time-out has been granted. Rule 6.02 [b] and [c]. Jose Canseco of the A's got called out on such a play during the 1992 season.

14

Leaning over the Plate

Neither. Instead, the umpire invoked Rule 6.08 [b] against Minoso: "If the ball is in the strike zone when it touches the batter, it shall be called a strike, whether or not the batter tries to avoid the ball."

Suppose in the same situation Minoso got hit by the pitch when he was standing six inches off the plate. Would it count as a hit-by-pitch or a walk? Answer: a walk.

The Sultan's Bat

No, it doesn't. Hack Miller of the 1922–23 Cubs claimed he used a 65-ounce bat. In those two seasons, the only ones in which he had a sufficient number of at-bats, he batted .352 and .301 respectively.

In 1923, he hit a career-high 20 homers.

Babe Ruth, the "Sultan of Swat," at times used a 52-ounce bat. He, of course, batted .342 lifetime and hit 714 career home runs.

Babe Herman, a .324 life-time hitter, swung a 48-ounce bat during his heyday of 1928–30, when he batted .340, .381, and .393, respectively, for the Brooklyn Dodgers. A Brooklyn teammate once asked Herman, "Why do you swing such a heavy bat?" Known for his quick rejoinders, Babe snapped, "If it's good enough for one Babe [Ruth], it's good enough for another Babe [Herman]." Herman hit a career-high 35 home runs in 1930.

16

The Way the Ball Bounces

A home run. The foul poles in all major-league parks today are placed in fair territory, behind the fence or wall. Thus, any batted ball that hits either the foul pole or the wire netting extending from it is a home run. Rule 2.00 a fair ball. Hayes's hit, a solo home run, gave the Yankees a 1-0 lead. They ultimately won, 3-0. However, the foul poles at major league parks were not always placed behind either the fence or wall. They were once situated in a groove or hollow that was inserted into the top of the fence or wall. If the batted ball struck the foul pole and bounded into the stands in foul territory, the batter was awarded a two-base hit; if the batted ball hit the foul pole and bounced over the fence in fair territory, the batter was awarded a home run; if the batted ball rebounded off the foul pole onto the playing field, it was in play and the batter had to run out his hit.

Swinging
Third Strike

No. To conclude a strikeout, the catcher must hold the third strike or pick up the loose ball and throw it to first base before the runner for the out to count. Henrich was safe at first base because he reached it before the throw. Rule 6.09 [b].

A "Heads-Up" Play

The umpire is right to rule a "bounding" fair ball that is deflected by a player into the stands in fair territory a double. Once a fly ball hits the fence, it is considered a "bounding" ball, not a ball "in flight," and cannot be ruled a home run. A ball "in flight"—that is, a fair fly ball deflected by a player into the stands in fair territory—is a home run.

The Expos' Andre Dawson, in a 1977 game at Montreal's Olympic Stadium, rocketed a long fly ball to center field that bounded off the wall, struck Dodger outfielder Rick Monday on the head, and bounced into the stands. Dawson got a double; Monday, a headache.

The Ground-Rule Triple

Baseball doesn't have a ground-rule triple today, but it once did. In the 1903 World Series between Pittsburgh and Boston, the Pirates, because of overflow crowds, permitted fans to stand behind a rope in the outfield. Both teams agreed that any

batted balls that rolled under
the rope would be called ground-rule triples.
In the four games played at Pittsburgh, the Red Sox
collected 12 of the 17 ground-rule triples. Tommy Leach of the
Pirates hit a record four three-base hits in this World Series.

Distracting the Batter

No, but it used to be, before Eddie Stanky of the New York Giants
brought undue attention to the play in the early 1950s. Today, the
umpire would stop play and warn the violator that if he continued
to try to distract the batter, he would be ejected from the game.
The Twins tried a similar tactic on Boggs, when he was on a hitting
streak in the mid-1980s. Second baseman Phil Lombardozzi and shortstop Phil Gagne changed positions just as the pitcher delivered the
ball to the plate. Umpire Ed Brinkman stopped play and
applied Rule 4.06 [b]. illegal distraction. On the
next pitch, Boggs hit a line-drive double.

19

Pine-Tar Play

Well, first they look at the rule book. When they find that this particular rule is not specifically covered by the text, they have to look up indirect references to help them form a conclusion. The references that they find are: 1) a batter will be out when he hits an illegally batted ball; 2) an illegally batted ball is one that is hit with a bat that does not conform to the rules; and 3) the bat handle may be covered with any foreign material, including pine tar, to improve the grip, as long as it does not exceed 18 inches from the knob to the barrel.

If, in the umpire's opinion, the foreign substance exceeds the 18-inch limit, the arbiter shall remove the bat from the game. Based upon that information, the umpires conclude that the bat was illegal and Munson is out. "A rule is a rule," they say, and the Yankees do not appeal.

Pine-Tar Reprise

Yes. He said that while the umpires' decision was technically correct, it wasn't in keeping with the "spirit of the rules." The game would have to be replayed with two out in the ninth inning. The rules say that a batter shall be declared out if a tampered bat increases the distance of a batted ball. Pine tar, it is said, does not add distance to a batted ball. Later in the season, the suspended game was completed. The Royals won, 4-3.

Chasing a Pitch

No, the home run is not legal. The batter must have both feet within the box when he makes contact with the ball. If he hits a ball with one, or both, of his feet outside of the box, he is considered to have hit the ball illegally, and he is called out. It is important to note, however, that if the batter misses the pitch, it is simply a strike and he continues to hit.

Hank Aaron lost a home

run in this fashion. He "chased" a pitch by Cardinal left-hander Curt Simmons and homered into an out. Aaron has an all-time high 755 career home runs. One more wouldn't have made too much difference.

Taking One for the Team

One, if the pitch was a strike. Two, if he didn't try to avoid the pitch. And three, if the pitch followed a balk with a runner or runners on base. Rule 6.08 [b].

Fist Ball

No. The batter is out, and the ball becomes dead as soon as it hits the batter. In order for it to have been a foul ball, it would have had to hit the bat before it hit the batter. A batter is out when he attempts to hit a third strike and the ball touches him. Rule 6.05 [7].

Is Sacrifice an At-Bat?

Yes, he does. Has the present rule always been in effect? No, it hasn't. It came into effect, in its present form, in 1908. Eighteen years later (1926), the sacrifice fly rule was amended so that a batter would be charged with no at-bat if any base runner advanced a base on a "fly-ball." In 1931, five years later, the sacrifice fly rule went out of effect until 1939, when it was reinstated in its initial form (no at-bat when a runner moves up) for just one year. There was no sacrifice fly rule from 1939 until 1954, when it was reintroduced in its present form.

Baseball is mostly a consistent game. But not the sacrifice fly rule, which has affected career batting averages. For example, Joe DiMaggio (1936–51) played only one year with the rule in effect. Hank Aaron (1954–76), on the other hand, played his entire career with the rule in effect. Lifetime, DiMaggio batted .325; Aaron, .305.

Managers' Quotes

1. Who said, of his team's home park: "When you come to the plate in this ballpark, you're in scoring position"?

2. Who made the egotistical comment, "Stay close in the early innings, and I'll think of something"?

3. What diminutive skipper said these fiery words: "I think there should be bad blood between all teams"?

4. What manager, saddled with an inept team, moaned, "Can't anyone here play this game?"

5. Who said, "You don't save a pitcher for tomorrow. Tomorrow it may rain"? Big clue: He's also famous for saying, "Nice guys finish last"–although that wasn't exactly what he said.

6. After suffering through a tough road trip, what 1997 Reds manager said, "When it rains it pours, and we're in the midst of a monsoon"?

a. Charlie Dressen
b. Don Baylor
c. Earl Weaver
d. Casey Stengel
e. Ray Knight
f. Leo Durocher

Answer on page 95.

Humor Match-Up

1. When told his salary was more than the earnings of President Hoover, who stated, "Oh, yeah? Well, I had a better year than he had"?

2. On his disdain for artificial grass, what slugger commented, "If a horse can't eat it, I don't want to play on it"?

3. When asked for the highlight of his career, which player responded, "I walked with the bases loaded to drive in the winning run in an intrasquad game in spring training"?

4. Although he probably wasn't trying to be humorous, this good ol' country boy once said, "They X-rayed my head and didn't find anything."

5. Speaking of his dislike for hitting in Comiskey Park, this player said, "At Wrigley Field, I feel like King Kong. Here, I feel like Donkey Kong."

a. Gary Gaetti
b. Bob Uecker
c. Babe Ruth
d. Dick Allen
e. Dizzy Dean

Answer on page 95.

25

PITCHING

The Trial Run

A Milwaukee Brewer relief pitcher comes into a game to face Cecil Fielder of the Tigers in the bottom of the seventh inning. Before the new hurler throws the first of his eight warm-up pitches, he spits on his hands. The home-plate umpire calls "Ball one," and warns the pitcher not to do it again.

But the Brewer hurler defies the umpire and spits on his hands again before he throws his second warm-up pitch. The umpire then ejects the pitcher. Brewer manager Phil Garner, who argued the first call from the bench, now charges the plate umpire and hotly contests the first and second calls. Does Garner have the rule book on his side?

Answer on page 36–37.

26

Balk Play

The Cardinals have runners on second and third after
Vince Coleman doubles Ozzie Smith to third base. Then the
Atlanta Braves pitcher balks Smith home and Coleman to third base.
Before the next pitch, however, the Braves first baseman calls for the ball,
steps on first base, and claims that Coleman missed that base while running
out his double. The umpire saw Coleman miss the base. How should he rule?

Answer on page 37.

27

A Fine Line

The Phillies have Dale Sveum, Lenny Dykstra, and John Kruk on third, second, and first bases, respectively, with one out, when Dale Murphy rips a
line drive back at the opposing pitcher. The pitcher drops the ball,
picks it up, and then initiates a pitcher-to-home-to-first double
play to end the inning. Or does he?

Answer on page 38.

Snap Throw

There are many present-day left-handed pitchers who come to a set position with a runner on first, step back off the pitcher's rubber with their pivot foot, and—without a step toward first base—throw to first base. Legal play?

Answer on page 38.

Pitch-o-Meters

28

Dennis Cook, a notoriously slow worker, is pitching for the Indians in a game in which Cleveland holds a 3-2 lead over the Blue Jays in the top half of the seventh inning. There are two out, no one on base, and Joe Carter is up at the plate with a full count on him. Cook shakes off a couple of signs, backs off the rubber, looks at his outfield alignment, gets back on the rubber, and stares interminably at the batter. Suddenly, the plate umpire jumps out from behind the plate and calls, "Ball four." Can he do that?

Answer on page 39.

Pick Off or Pick Up?

With the bases loaded, the hurler tries to pick off the runner on first base instead of pitching to the plate. But the ball sails wildly into the first-base seats. How far can the runners advance?

Answer on page 40.

The Booted Play

29

The San Francisco Giants have Willie McGee on second base, Will Clark on first base, and Matt Williams at the plate, while the host Cubs have relief pitcher Dave Smith on the mound. Smith's first pitch to Williams bounces in front of the plate and off the Bruin backstop's shin guard towards the first-base dugout. McGee and Clark move up a base on the wild pitch. But the Cubs catcher, in running down the ball, accidentally kicks it into the Cubs' dugout. What's the ruling? Can runners advance only one base on a wild pitch?

Answer on page 40–41.

The
Sidewinder

The pitcher is in the stretch position. With his foot on the side of the rubber, he pitches to the batter. Is there anything wrong with this?

Answer on page 41.

 30

Stretching
the Rules

Some pitchers like to work from the stretch in one continuous motion. The umpires "look the other way" as long as no one complains. But one day a batter got upset with the motion, so the umpires enforced the balk rule. What exactly is the rule?

Answer on page 42–43.

Balk Talk

With Paul Molitor of the Brewers at first base, the
Tiger pitcher—in the set-position stance, with the ball in his
glove and his pitching arm at his side—takes his sign, removes the
ball from his glove, and moves to the set position.
Good move?

Answer on page 43.

31

In Front of the Runner

Let's take the preceding situations one step further. Molitor is now at
second base. The Tiger pitcher, anticipating that Molitor is going to attempt
to steal third, takes his stretch and comes to a stop. Then, as the Brewer
infielder breaks for the advance bag, he throws to third baseman
Tony Phillips for the "out."
Is Molitor out?

Answer on page 44.

The Faux Pas

Delino DeShields is on first base for the Expos with Larry Walker at the plate. The Chicago Cubs pitcher, in the set position, quickly steps off the rubber with his pivot foot and fires the ball towards the plate. Walker hits the ball over the wall at Wrigley Field for an apparent two-run homer. Does the run count?

Answer on page 44.

The Spitball Rule

The Mets have the bases loaded in a game against the visiting Astros. Eddie Murray is the batter with a three-two count in a 3-3 game. Before the Astro reliever delivers the pay-off pitch on this balmy night, he holds the ball up to his mouth and blows on it, and then fires a pitch that Murray swings through for strike three.

The game goes to extra innings. Or does it?

Answer on page 45.

Who Gets the Save?

During the 1992 season, Jeff Reardon of the Red Sox broke Rollie Fingers' former all-time career record for saves (341). In a late-season game, Boston was leading its opposition, 6-3. Reardon came to the mound with two runners on base and two out in the top half of the ninth inning. On one pitch he retired the batter to nail down a victory for the BoSox. Did he get credited with a save?

Answer on page 45–46.

The Good-Hitting Pitcher

One day in 1977, Ken Brett of the White Sox was the starting pitcher, and Brian Downing, the designated hitter. Brett pitched well for seven innings, but in the eighth, he ran into trouble. It was time for a change. White Sox manager Bob Lemon knew that. But he didn't want to remove

Brett entirely from the game, because Brett was a good hitter (in 1973 he had hit home runs in four consecutive games—a record for pitchers). The opposing pitcher was an effective right-hander. Downing was also a righthander. Lemon switched Brett to first base. Did this affect the batting order?

Answer on page 46.

34 Automatic Intentional Pass?

Increasingly, there is talk these days about speeding up the game. Enforcing the 20-second pitch rule would be one way to do it. Putting a more stringent time limit on in-between-inning radio and television commercials would be the most practical way to do it (but we know that's not going to happen!). Giving automatic intentional passes would be a third way to speed up the game. But there are at least six good reasons why an automatic intentional pass might not be good for baseball. Can you list them?

Answer on page 47.

More Managers

1. Even after winning a World Series in the 1990s, this manager muttered, "I'm not sure whether I'd rather be managing or testing bulletproof vests."

2. This man's team was injury plagued in 1989, prompting him to observe, "If World War III broke out, I'd guarantee you we'd win the pennant by 20 games. All our guys would be 4-F. They couldn't pass the physical."

3. In 1997, this White Sox skipper griped, "I learned a long time ago, in this game you might as well take the blame because you're going to get it anyway."

4. His pitcher entered the game with the bases loaded. Two wild pitches later, the bases were empty because all three men had scored, leading to this managerial quip: "Well, that's one way to pitch out of a bases-loaded jam." Clue: He was managing the Brewers when this occurred.

a. Terry Bevington

b. Tom Trebelhorn

c. Whitey Herzog

d. Joe Torre

Answer on page 95.

35

PITCHING ANSWERS

The Trial Run

Today he does. But if the incident had happened before the 1969 season, he wouldn't. In fact, it was a situation in 1968 that prompted league officials to amend this rule.

36   In a game at Shea Stadium, John Boozer of the Phillies came into the contest in the bottom of the seventh inning to replace Woody Fryman. Before Boozer took his first warm-up pitch, he spat on his hands. Plate umpire Ed Vargo called "Ball one."

At this point Phillie manager Gene Mauch charged out of the Philadelphia dugout and ordered Boozer to repeat his act. Boozer did. Vargo, who could have ejected Boozer there, called "Ball two." Mauch insisted that Boozer repeat his ritual. The pitcher did—and was promptly ejected by

Vargo. Some minutes later, Mauch was ejected, too. The three ball calls stood. Dick Hall came into the game—with a 3-0 count—to pitch to Mets batter Buddy Harrelson.

Gene Mauch lost the argument but won a point by bringing attention to a foolish rule. After the season, it was removed by the rules committee. Pitchers can now spit on their hands before throwing warm-up pitches.

Balk Play

He should deny the appeal. Even though no pitch had been made since Coleman's double, the rule states that an appeal must be made before the "next pitch or any play or attempted play." The balk constitutes a play. Rule 7.10 [d], paragraph beginning "Any appeal."

A Fine Line

There is a fine line in this situation. It's a judgment call on the part of the umpire. He has to determine whether the pitcher purposefully or accidentally dropped the ball.

On May 20, 1960, this exact play happened in a game between the Reds and the Cardinals. Joe Nuxhall was the Reds pitcher; Stan Musial, the batter for the Cards. Umpire Ed Vargo ruled that Nuxhall dropped the ball on purpose. (Remember, no infield fly rule can be called on a line drive.) Musial was declared out and the ball dead, and the umpire ordered the runners to return to their original bases. Rule 6.05 [l].

Snap Throw

Yes, provided that the pitcher's pivot foot, in stepping back, touches the ground before he separates his hands. Rule 8.01 [e]. Dave Righetti, when he pitched with the Yankees, was one of the popularizers of this move.

Pitch-o-Meters

Rule 8.04 says he can. The pitcher must deliver the ball to the hitter, when the bases are unoccupied, within 20 seconds after he gets the ball. Each violation of this rule will result in a ball call.

The 20-second rule is rarely called. The umpire just has too many things to do to count 20 seconds or consult a watch. However, if the pitcher is a notoriously slow worker, the umpire might decide to clock the hurler.

Joe Cronin, when president of the American League, decided to get tough on pitchers who stalled on the mound. In 1969, he told each club that it had to install a "pitch-o-meter" on the scoreboard. But only the Indians and White Sox went along with Cronin's edict, and the crackdown soon subsided. It went the way of many baseball fads, as, for example, get-tough policies on pitchers who balk.

Pick Off or Pick Up?

Each runner can advance one base. The rule is one base if the pitcher was on the rubber. If he had stepped off the rubber and thrown the ball into the stands, he would have been penalized two bases per runner. If he had taken a return throw from the catcher, in front of the rubber, and hurled the ball into the first-base stands, he also would have been penalized two bases per runner.

Chuck Stobbs of the 1956 Senators found himself in the hurler's situation. Pitching to the Tigers' Bob Kennedy, with his pivot foot on the rubber, he "picked off" a fan in the first-base boxes. Each runner "picked up" a base on the play.

The Booted Play

Yes, runners may advance only one base on a wild pitch that goes into dead territory. However, if the wild-pitch ball remains on the playing field, and is subsequently kicked or deflected into dead territory, the runners shall be awarded two bases from the position the runners were in at the time of the pitch. Rule 7.05 [h] approved ruling. McGee scores and Clark advances to third.

Early in the 1992 season, a Yankee catcher inadvertently made this faux pas.

The Sidewinder

The pitcher has just committed a balk. According to the rule book, the "set position" is indicated by the pitcher when he stands facing the batter with his entire foot on, or in front of, and in contact with, not off the end of, the pitcher's plate, holding the ball in both hands in front of his body and coming to a complete stop. The key wording here is "not off the end of the pitcher's plate."

Steve Blass of the winning Pirates was charged with this type of balk in the 1979 World Series. The umpire thought he was doing it too frequently, but he was still the recipient of a tough call.

Stretching
the Rules

The umpires don't always agree on a balk. The pitcher, working from the stretch, must come to a set position before he releases the ball. That's what the rule book says.

In the early 1950s, a plate umpire called a record four balks on Yankee pitcher Vic Raschi in one game. Raschi didn't like to come to a stop position. After the umpire had called the first balk, Raschi became stubborn. The pitcher wanted to see how far the umpire would go. Raschi stopped committing balks only when manager Casey Stengel warned him that one more infraction would cost him money.

Allie Reynolds, who also didn't like to come to a stop position, pitched the next day. When the first runner against him reached base, Reynolds paid undue attention to him. The pitcher kept throwing to first base. Minutes went by. But he refused to deliver the ball to the plate. Finally the fans got restless. They began to boo.

The plate umpire got restless, too. He visited the mound and asked Reynolds why he wasn't pitching to the batter. Reynolds said he was afraid that if he pitched the ball, the umpire would call a balk.

That ended the balk calls. Raschi and Reynolds continued to pitch to the plate in one fluid motion.

Balk Talk

No, it's a balk. Suppose instead, the pitcher receives the ball from his catcher and, with his feet in the set-position stance, nervously bounces the ball in his glove a few times or removes the ball from his glove. Balk?

Yes. In both cases. The limitations on a pitcher's movements start when he intentionally contacts the rubber with his pivot foot.

Rule 8.01 [a] and [b].

In Front of
the Runner

Yes, provided the Tiger moundsman did not start a pitch after his stretch-and-stop. Suppose Molitor had not been running on the play?

The pitcher can't throw to an unoccupied base. If he does, it is a balk. Rule 8.05 [d].

The Faux Pas

No. The pitcher's action was a balk. Rule 8.05 [e]. Once he disengaged his foot from the rubber, he became an infielder. A batter can't hit an infielder's throw. If the batter had hit the offering by the pitcher while he had his pivot foot on the rubber, the Expos could have elected to take the two-run homer in place of the balk. But in the above example, it is a balk. DeShields would advance to second base, and the count on Walker would remain the same.

The Spitball Rule

No. The game ends right there. As soon as the pitcher brings the ball to his mouth, the umpire calls a ball on the pitcher. Murray walks and the winning run is forced home. The pitcher may not bring the ball to his mouth, except when the weather is cold and both managers, before the game, agree to waive the rule. The first time the pitcher does it, the umpire may award a ball to the batter. The second time the pitcher does it, the umpire may eject him from the game. Rule 8.02 [a].

Who Gets the Save?

Yes, he did. In order to qualify for a save, a relief pitcher must satisfy one of the following three conditions: 1) His team must have been leading by no more than three runs—and he must have pitched effectively—when he entered the game; or 2) When he entered the game, the tying run must have been on base, on deck, or at bat; or 3) He must have effectively pitched three or more innings. Rule 10.20. Reardon qualified under conditions one and two.

In another late-season game in 1992, Dennis Eckersley of the Oakland A's picked up a save under similar circumstances. He was embarrassed, though. The "save" was too cheap, he said. Everything's relative. In 1973 play, for example, a relief pitcher would have been credited with a save for "saving" a 15-3 rout.

The Good-Hitting Pitcher

Yes, it did affect things. Now Lemon had 10 batters in the lineup. Once the game pitcher is switched from the mound to a defensive position, this move shall terminate the DH role for the rest of the game. Rule 6.10 [b]. Downing had to be taken out of the lineup. (The game pitcher may only pinch-hit for the DH.)

Automatic
Intentional Pass?

One, there could be a passed ball. Two, there could be a wild pitch. Three, the backstop could step out of the batter's box too early and get called for a catcher's balk. Four, the batter could reach out and hit a pitch too close to the plate and drive it for a game-winning blow. Five, the batter could step either on the plate or over it in trying to hit the ball, and subsequently be called out. Six, the fans would be deprived of an opportunity to boo the pitcher! Nothing major.

BASEBALL QUOTABLE

Ex-pitcher turned announcer Dizzy Dean would butcher the English language. In one case, he said a player had "slud into third" instead of "slid." Another remark was, "Don't fail to miss tomorrow's game."

FIELDING

The Trick That Backfired

The hidden-ball trick has to be done just right in order for it to work. It also has to be done correctly to avoid a balk being called. Take the following case, for example.

48

On August 12, 1961, San Francisco Giant shortstop Jose Pagan decided that he was going to pull the hidden-ball trick when Cincinnati catcher Johnny Edwards was on second base. He hid the ball in his glove and waited for Edwards to step off the base. In the meantime, pitcher Jack Sanford strode to the mound, pretending that he had the ball. The second-base umpire was on the ball, though. He called a balk against Sanford. Why?

Answer on page 60.

You've Got to
Run 'Em Out

In a 1992 game between the White Sox and the host Yankees, New York's Randy Velarde singles to right field, a run scoring on the play. Dan Pasqua's relay throw misses the cutoff man, however, and Velarde continues on to second base on the play.

When catcher Carlton Fisk realizes that there is no White Sox teammate backing up the play, he races to retrieve the ball as it rolls toward the visitors' third-base dugout. At the last possible second, he slides feet-first into the dugout in order to stop and recover the ball. Ultimately, he takes firm possession of the ball, which had come to rest on the top step of the dugout.

Velarde, who thinks that the ball has gone into dead territory, and that he is entitled to a free base, trots to third base, but Fisk now steps out of the dugout and throws the ball to third baseman Robin Ventura for an easy tag-out. The Yankees don't protest the call.

Should they have?

Answer on page 60–61.

49

Unaware

In August 1970, the Reds were leading the host Pirates in the bottom of the fourth inning. But the Pirates had runners on first and third with two out, and Fred Norman had a three-two count on batter Omar Moreno. On the payoff pitch Lee Lacy at first was off-and-running from first base. Catcher Johnny Bench instinctively threw the ball to shortstop Davey Concepcion, who applied the tag to the sliding Lacy. The umpire called Lacy out.

50 Lacy, thinking his side was out, then got up and walked toward the first-base line, waiting to be delivered his glove for the field. Lacy was unaware that the pitch to Moreno had been wide and high for ball four. He had been forced to advance on the walk. When his teammates yelled that fact to him, and that he should return to second, Concepcion was waiting for him at the bag with the ball. The umpire called Lacy out for the second time.

Pirate manager Chuck Tanner argued the call for a long time. Did his argument prevail?

Answer on page 61.

Is it Legal?

In a game at the Oakland Coliseum, Kelly Gruber of the Blue Jays hits a soft pop foul towards the third-box seats. The A's third baseman, Carney Lansford, makes a running catch about 10 feet from the boxes, but his momentum carries him into the wire protecting fence, the ball dropping out of his glove upon contact. Is it a legal catch?

Answer on page 61–62.

Oldie but Goodie

51

Here's a situation that's frequently talked about but rarely happens. A high pop-up follows a mortar-like trajectory. A bevy of infielders, including the pitcher, settle under the ball. Confusion concerning who is going to make the catch leads to the ball falling safely to the ground. As a matter of fact, it hits the mound on the third base side, and the slope of the mound causes the ball to carom foul about halfway between home plate and third base. What's your call?

Answer on page 62–63.

Classic Blunder

In post-season play, here's a memorable play from Game 1 of the 1996 American League Championship Series between the Baltimore Orioles and the New York Yankees. With Baltimore up by one run at 4-3 in the bottom of the eighth, Derek Jeter drilled the ball to right field. It appeared that the ball had just enough oomph to carry it into the stands for a homer. Still, the Orioles' outfielder, Tony Tarasco, was camped under the ball; he clearly felt he had a chance at making the catch. However, a 12-year-old fan snared the ball, and the umpire, Rich Garcia, had to make the call. What should his ruling be?

Answer on page 63–64.

Is it Interference?

Another famous play in the American League Championship Series came in 1998. The Yankees again were the host team, this time facing the Cleveland Indians in Game 2. The twelfth inning rolled around and the teams were deadlocked at one run apiece.

Cleveland had Enrique Wilson on first base when Travis Fryman laid down a sacrifice bunt to move the potential winning run into scoring position. The Yankees' first baseman, Tino Martinez, gloved the ball and threw for second baseman Chuck Knoblauch, who was covering first on the play.

Fryman, meanwhile, was running inside the first-base foul line, not inside the three-foot lane that runs the last 45 feet from home to first in foul ground. Runners are required to be within that path on plays like this one. When the Martinez throw ricocheted off Fryman and rolled away, the ump called Fryman safe. Knoblauch felt the ump should have ruled Fryman out for interference, and became so incensed that he forgot to chase down the ball. This allowed Wilson to romp around the bases and score, and Fryman to put down anchor at third base.

Now, your challenge is this: is a runner automatically out when struck by a ball in such a scenario?

Answer on page 64.

53

Eight Men on
the Field

Marty Barrett of the Red Sox hits very few home runs. Understandably, he was very upset when the Yankees' Ken Griffey dived into the left-field stands at Yankee Stadium to rob the Boston second-sacker of a four-base blast. Can an outfielder leave the playing field to make a catch?

Answer on page 65.

The Infield (?) Fly

The Tigers, with men on second and first, have no out in the top of the eighth inning. The batter lofts a soft fly ball behind second base. The center fielder of the Brewers comes in; the second baseman goes out. Either one of them can catch the ball easily.

When the umpire sees the second baseman settle under the ball, he calls the batter automatically out on the infield fly rule. But the fielder drops the ball, and other players on the field become confused. The runner on second, believing the batter is safe on the error, runs to third, thinking that he is forced. The second baseman's throw beats him to the base, but the third baseman commits an error, too. He doesn't tag the runner. Instead, he steps on third for the "force."

Three questions: 1) Can an umpire call the infield fly rule when the defensive man is in the outfield? 2) Is the runner called back from third base? 3) Who gets charged with errors on the play?

Answer on page 66–67.

55

Learn the Tricky Infield Fly Rule

The Yankees have runners on third, second, and first bases, respectively, when Don Mattingly hits a high pop fly towards the Indian first baseman. The umpire calls, "Infield fly, if fair." All of the runners stay close to their bases.

Knowing the rules, the first baseman lets

the ball fall to the ground
untouched. But he catches the ball on the first
bounce and steps on first base. Not conversant with the
rule, the runner steps off the bag and is tagged by the first baseman. In the meantime, the runner at third bolts for the plate and is
thrown out by a toss from the first baseman to the catcher. Triple play?

Answer on page 67.

Knockdown

56

Terry Pendleton of the Braves is on first base when David Justice
lashes a single to right field. Pendleton rounds second widely and continues
to third as the Cincinnati Reds right fielder unleashes a wide throw to the
outfield side of the third base. Third baseman Chris Sabo, in trying to
field the ball, runs into Pendleton and knocks him to the ground. Is
defensive interference called? Does any defensive player receive
an error? Where do Pendleton and Justice end up?

Answer on page 68.

Misuse of Mask

Mike Scioscia, the longtime catcher for the Los Angeles Dodgers, had a "Murphy's Law" year in 1992. If anything could go wrong, it did. Take this play, for example.

The host San Diego Padres were trailing the Los Angeles Dodgers in the bottom of the eighth inning, 3-2, when San Diego rallied. With Tony Fernandez on second base and two out, Tony Gwynn singled to right field to tie the score, and on the throw to the plate, he advanced to second base.

In the meantime, Scioscia bobbled the skip throw from the outfield, and then reached out with his right hand—which held his mask—and scooped up the free ball into his mitt.

Instantaneously, San Diego manager Greg Riddoch charged home plate and demanded that Fernandez score from second base on Scioscia's catcher's interference. Did the Padres pilot have a valid point?

Answer on page 68.

57

Don't Catch It!

In the bottom of the ninth inning, in a game between the Cardinals and the host Pirates, Andy Van Slyke, who represents the game-winning run, is at third base with one out. Batter Barry Bonds hits a long foul fly ball down the left-field line. The ball is hit deep enough to score the winning run. The Redbird left fielder knows this, so he deliberately lets the ball fall untouched to the ground. Does he receive an error on this play?

Answer on page 69.

58

Teamwork

The Red Sox have a runner at third base, and one out. The batter hits a long fly ball to right center against the Yankee pitcher. The ball deflects off the right fielder's glove and floats into the center fielder's mitt. Two questions: 1) Is the batter out? 2) Can the runner tag up after the ball touches the right fielder's glove?

Answer on page 69.

Managers,
Last Call

1. Lucky enough to be George Brett's manager, this man was asked what he told Brett regarding hitting. The Royals manager replied, "I tell him, 'Attaway to hit, George.' "

2. Never known for his use of grammar, this great manager once said of a player's injury, "There's nothing wrong with his shoulder except some pain, and pain don't hurt you."

3. On what it takes to be a successful manager, an all-time big-name manager opined, "A sense of humor and a good bullpen."

4. Two quotes from the same guy: A) "I'm not the manager because I'm always right, but I'm always right because I'm the manager." B) "The worst thing about managing is the day you realize you want to win more than your players do."

5. This manager-for-a-day naively believed, "Managing isn't all that difficult. Just score more runs than the other guy."

a. Ted Turner
b. Whitey Herzog
c. Gene Mauch

d. Jim Frey
e. Sparky Anderson

Answer on page 95.

59

FIELDING
ANSWERS

The Trick That Backfired

The pitcher, without the ball, cannot stand either on or astride the mound. Rule 8.05 [i].

A more celebrated case occurred when Dick Groat of the Cardinals, in the fourth game of the 1964 World Series, pulled the hidden ball trick against Mickey Mantle of the Yankees at second base. That play worked because Roger Craig, the Redbird pitcher, fiddled in the playing area off the pitcher's mound before and during the time that Groat applied the tag.

You've Got to Run 'Em Out

No. A fielder or catcher may reach or step into, or go into, the dugout with one or both feet to make

60

a catch (play), and if he holds
the ball, the catch (play) shall be allowed.
The ball is in play. Rule 7.04 [c].

Unaware

No. When it didn't, he protested the game. But National League President Chub Feeney overruled it on two grounds: one, there had been no misinterpretation of rules, and two, Lacy should have known what was going on.

Is It Legal?

It's a matter of judgment on the umpire's part. The rule book says that if the fielder has contact with another fielder or wall immediately following his contact with the ball—and drops it—it is not a legal catch. Rule 2.00 catch. Ten feet would seem to be a considerable distance, but it wasn't in the following application.

Late in the 1992 season, the host Braves were leading the Padres when San Diego's

Gene Richards, with no one on and two out, sent a twisting fly ball down the left-field line. Terry Harper made a running catch inside the foul line, but his momentum carried him across the line into the bullpen railing. Trying to cushion his landing, he grabbed the railing but dropped the ball. Umpire Ed Vargo called the play a no-catch, and by the time Harper retrieved the ball and returned it to the infield, Richards had circled the bases.

The official scorer ruled the play a four-base error, but the National League office overruled the scoring and called the play an inside-the-park home run.

Oldie but Goodie

Since no fielder touched the ball in fair territory, the ball is treated the same as if it had been a slow roller that settled in foul territory. It's merely a foul ball.

This play actually happened on August 7, 1999, when the Giants' J.T. Snow launched the pop-up. Several players converged on the ball, but second baseman Brett Boone called for it. He was unable to make the play, and the ball fell to earth, hitting the mound.

One report said the infielders looked like a bunch of Little Leaguers letting the ball drop. Still, some credit must go to the shortstop, Ozzie Guillen, who alertly turned a defensive blunder into a harmless foul ball. When he saw the path the ball began to take after hitting the mound, he let it go, waited until it crossed the foul line, then pounced on the ball, killing the play.

Classic Blunder

The rule states that if the ball is over the fence and a fan touches it, the hitter gets his home run. If a fan reaches over the field and touches the ball, forget the home run, it's fan interference. In this case, Garcia perceived the ball was already into the stands, so he gave Jeter the homer, tying the game.

Replays, however, showed

he had blown the call.

Indeed, Garcia himself, upon seeing the replays, admitted he had been wrong. That didn't placate the seething Orioles, especially since the Yankees went on to win the opener 5–4 in 11 innings.

The O's rebounded to take the second game, but were swept over in the last three games, and the Yankees went on to win the World Series.

Is It Interference?

64

According to the rules, he is not automatically out even if he wasn't running in the proper lane; it's a judgment call. Some experts say Fryman didn't interfere because he actually beat the ball to the bag. In other words, he was already safe when the ball struck him, so he had a right to be where he was at that moment. Two things remain certain on that play: 1) it was a tough call and 2) Knoblauch should have hustled first and asked questions later (something he readily admitted after the game).

Eight Men on the Field

Yes, an outfielder, or any other player, can leave the playing field to make a catch. The determining factor is whether the fielder's momentum carries him into the stands while he is making the play. If it does, it is a good catch. If the player establishes a stationary position in the stands before he makes the catch, however, the grab is disallowed.

In this situation, however, Griffey timed his jump perfectly and made a sensational catch while bouncing off a fan who was trying to snatch the ball from him. It was a legitimate catch.

If Griffey had mistimed his jump, landed in the stands early, and then caught Barrett's drive, the hit would have been ruled a home run.

But Griffey played the ball perfectly. Only his landing, back on the playing field, was a little less than smooth. Dave Winfield, playing the part of an Olympic judge, gave Griffey a ten on his dive, but only a five on his landing.

The Infield (?) Fly

First, the umpire can call the infield fly rule on an outfield play. The rule permits the umpire to make the call any time the infielder can make the play with ordinary effort. Second, the runner on third base is not called back to second. In an infield fly play, the runner can advance at his own risk. Third, there were two errors on the play: one of commission (the second baseman's) and one of omission (the third baseman's). However, since the second baseman's error confused the runner into running, he is charged with a miscue by the official scorer.

A similar play occurred in a 1956 game between the Braves and the Pirates. The Braves, with Frank Torre at bat, had Bobby Thomson on second and Bill Bruton on first. Pirate Dick Groat, an MVP winner four years later, dropped the ball and threw it to third baseman Gene Freese in time for the out. But Freese didn't tag Thomson; so the runner at third was safe, and Bruton moved up to second on the play.

66

There were three errors on the play: Groat's, Thomson's, and Freese's. But only Groat got officially charged with one. The Pirates won the game, though, 3-1.

Learn the Tricky Infield Fly Rule

Yes. All the runners were mixed up. First of all, the first baseman didn't have to touch first. The batter was already out on the infield fly. But the first baseman's act of touching first base confused the runner on first into thinking that he was forced to advance on the play. The runner, of course, advanced at his own risk after the infield fly was caught, so he became the second out. The runner at third, also advancing at his own risk, became the third out of the inning.

Rule 2.00 infield fly.

Knockdown

Sabo is charged with obstruction (Rule 7.06a) and picks up an error on the play. Pendleton and Justice are each awarded an advance base, Pendleton to score and Justice to second.

Misuse of Mask

Yes, he did. Each runner, including the batter-runner, may, without liability to be put out, advance two bases, if a fielder deliberately touches a thrown ball with his cap, mask, or any part of his uniform detached from its proper place on his person. The ball is in play. Rule 7.04 [d].

A similar play was called against Mike Heath when he was catching for the Tigers in the late 1980s. On a late throw from the out-field to the plate, the ball took a bad bounce to Heath's right, and he reached out with his mask in his right hand and caught it. The batter-runner, who had reached second base on the throw to the plate, was allowed to score.

Don't Catch It!

No. An error shall not be charged against any fielder who permits a foul fly to fall safe with a runner on third base before two are out if in the scorer's judgment the fielder deliberately refuses to catch in order that the runner on third shall not score after the catch. Rule 10.14 [e].

Teamwork

1) A fly ball that is deflected off one outfielder's glove into another's is a legal out. The batter is out. 2) A runner can legally tag up and advance as soon as a fielder touches the ball. He does not have to wait until a fielder "possesses" the ball.

On a play just like this, at Yankee Stadium in the late 1950s, Hank Bauer got the assist and Mickey Mantle, the putout. There was no runner on third. The batter got "put out."

BASE RUNNING

The "Wild Hoss"

They didn't call John Leonard Roosevelt "Pepper" Martin the "Wild Hoss of the Osage" for nothing. Martin used to run wild on the bases. In the 1931 and 1934 World Series, for example, Martin stole five and two bases, respectively—all of them, by the way, off Hall-of-Fame catcher Mickey Cochrane. Martin's team, the Cardinals, won the World Series both of these years.

Martin liked to "cut the pie," that is, show off from time to time. His big moment came during the 1933 season when he hit a home run over the fence, and proceeded to run the bases in reverse order! Is that legal?

Answer on page 78.

70

Lines Are Lines

David Cone is pitching for the Mets. Mackey Sasser is
the catcher. Cone blows the batter away with a swinging strike
on a hard slider that goes down and away, but Sasser has trouble
holding onto the pitch and it bounces about five feet to his right.
Since there is no one on base and no one out, the batter runs out the
play, but in running the last half of the distance from home to first, he runs
"outside" of the three-foot line, and Sasser's throw to first baseman Eddie
Murray hits him and bounces down the right-field line. The batter
goes to second base on the play. Does he have to give up his base?

Answer on page 79.

71

Two for the Price of One

John Kruk of the Phillies hits what appears to be a certain
double-play ball to Jose Lind, the Pirates' second baseman. Lind fields the ball cleanly and gives a

perfect toss to shortstop Jay Bell, who has enough time to take two full steps to touch second on the right-field side of the base. But before Bell can relay the ball to first for the inning-ending double play, the base runner from first veers deliberately out of his path to take out Bell, preventing him from making the throw. What's the umpire's call, if any?

Answer on page 79–80.

72

Indecisive Runner

The Brewers have a runner on first base when the batter bunts a ball toward Royal first baseman Wally Joyner. Noticing that the Milwaukee batter is not running out the play, Joyner allows the ball to bounce, picks it up, steps on first, and tags the runner who is trying to return to first. Good play?

Answer on page 80.

The Silent Speaker

In a game at the Astrodome, Phillies' Mike Schmidt is up with runners on first and second. He hits a tremendous blast that strikes the bottom side of a loudspeaker suspended 117 feet in the air in center field, 329 feet from home plate. What does the umpire call?

Answer on page 81.

Hit Behind a Fielder

73

Suppose the Cubs have the bases loaded with one out in the top of the ninth. The Cardinals, down by one run, bring their infield in. The batter hits a hard grounder to the right of the shortstop. The ball goes past his outstretched glove and hits the runner from second, who is behind the shortstop. The ball caroms off the runner's knee and rolls down the left-field line into foul territory. Three runners score, and the batter ends up on second. Do the runs count?

Answer on page 81–82.

Who's on Third?

The Yankees are at bat with one out and the bases loaded. Boston's pitcher hurls a fast ball right down the center of the plate, and the batter rockets it off the left-center-field fence. The ball bounces back towards the left fielder. The runner at third scores easily. The runner at second takes a wide turn at third, hesitates, and for some reason, returns to the bag. The runner at first sees the traffic jam at third and slides into the base. The batter, who has been running hard all the way, but with his head down, races into third with a stand-up "triple."

The Red Sox third baseman is confused, too, when he gets the throw from the left fielder. He knows that two of the runners don't belong there. But he doesn't know which two. So he does the obvious: he tags all three runners. The umpire calls two of them out. But which two? Who do you think has the right to be there?

Answer on page 82–83.

74

The Unkindest Touch

The Mets have a runner on second base, one out, and Eddie Murray at the plate in a game against the host Phillies. Murray lofts a soft fly ball to left-center field. The runner, thinking that the ball might drop for a base hit, goes half way to third, but the center fielder makes a good running catch.

His subsequent throw to third base, however, strikes a stone and bounces wildly past the third baseman into the Mets dugout. The runner from second advances two bases on the play, scoring a run. *But* he doesn't retouch second before he makes his advance.

The Phillies realize this, so the pitcher, when he puts the ball in play, throws it first to second base and files an appeal with the umpire. Is the run taken off the scoreboard?

Answer on page 83.

A Risky Play

A Cleveland runner is at second base when Brook
Jacoby swings at a Tim Leary pitch and is obstructed by the
Yankee catcher. But Jacoby still manages to line a single to left field.
The runner at second didn't get a good jump on the play, because there
was a chance that Yankee third baseman Charlie Hayes might snag the liner,
but he attempts to score anyway. However, left fielder Roberto Kelly whips
a strong throw to the plate and guns down the Indian runner.
Is the play called back because of the catcher's obstruction?

Answer on page 83.

76

BASEBALL QUOTABLE

Peppery manager Earl Weaver would upstage umpires
every chance he got. One day, taking a rule book out
on the field with him, he stated, "There ain't no rule in
the rule book about bringing a rule book on the field."

More Humor

1. Who said: "I've never played with a pitcher who tried to hit a batter in the head. Most pitchers are like me. If I'm going to hit somebody, I'm going to aim for the bigger parts"?
2. During his first ride to Wrigley Field after breaking into the majors, this West Virginia native spotted Lake Michigan and asked, "What ocean is that?"
3. Who was Dante Bichette referring to when he said: "He's the kid who, when he played Little League, all the parents called the president of the league and said, 'Get him out of there, I don't want him to hurt my son.' I had my mom call the National League office to see if she could do it for me"?
4. What player was former pitcher Darold Knowles talking about when he uttered these words: "There isn't enough mustard in the world to cover him"?
5. Who said: "We live by the Golden Rule—those who have the gold make the rules"?

a. Bert Blyleven
b. Buzzi Bavasi
c. John Kruk

d. Mark McGwire
e. Reggie Jackson

Answer on page 95.

BASERUNNING ANSWERS

The "Wild Hoss"

No, it isn't. Up until 1921 it was, though. After the 1920 season, the rule book was amended to read, "Running the bases in reverse order for the purpose either of confusing the fielders or making a travesty of the game is prohibited." Rule 7.02 and 7.10 [b]. When he reached home plate, Martin was called out.

Thirty years later, in 1963, another zany player, Jimmy Piersall, who was winding down his career with the equally zany Mets of that era, hit his 100th career home run one day and decided to celebrate the event in memorable fashion: he ran the bases in reverse order. But he was not called out. The play hadn't happened in so long that the umpires forgot the rule. Piersall's circuitous route that day brought so much media attention to the rule that no player since has attempted to follow in his footsteps.

Lines Are Lines

Yes, he is called out because he has interfered with Sasser's throw. The only time a batter can run inside or outside the three-foot line is when he is trying to avoid a fielder trying to play a batted ball. Rule 6.05 [k].

A few years back, the same play occurred in a Mariner–Yankee game at Yankee Stadium. Don Slaught was the Yank catcher, Don Mattingly the first baseman. The Seattle batter-runner was called out for interference.

Two for the Price of One

The umpire calls the batter out because of the runner's interference. Rule 6.05 [m]. This play has happened thousands of times in the major leagues. Today the umpires are more likely to penalize the flagrant runner. At one time, it was merely considered part of the game.

In 1949, for example, the Yankees

thought that the Red Sox were roughing up their shortstop, Phil Rizzuto. One day, in retaliation, Joe DiMaggio slid directly at Red Sox shortstop Vern Stephens, who was well out of the base path, to break up a double play. Stephens made no throw to first and the umpire assessed no penalty against DiMaggio and the batter-runner.

DiMaggio's slide had a twofold result: the runner ended up safe at first and the Red Sox left Rizzuto alone from that day forward. Today, it's different.

Indecisive Runner

Excellent! : a legal double play. Rule 6.05 [l] approved ruling.

In 1949, Yankee first baseman Tommy Henrich, who was a "heads-up player," fielded such a bunt by Washington Senator outfielder Buddy Stewart with Eddie Yost on first base. "Old Reliable" turned the one-hop bunt into a double play.

The Silent Speaker

The Astros do not have a ground rule, or an air rule, for that situation. The ball is "in play." The runners must advance at least one base because of the force play that is in effect. Beyond that, they advance at their own risk.

When Schmidt hit that "tape-measure" blast at the Astrodome with Dave Cash and Larry Bowa on base, the ball bounced straight down and center fielder Cesar Cedeno fielded it on a bounce. Schmidt got credited only with a long single! The runners each moved up only one base.

Hit Behind a Fielder

Yes, the runs do count. When the runner *behind* the fielder gets struck with a batted ball, the ball is live and in play if, in the umpire's judgment, no other fielder had a chance to make a play on the ball. In this case, the runs score and the batter is allowed to stay at second.

The Reds, in a game against the

Padres, had a similar situation. They had Johnny Bench on third, George Foster on second, and Dave Concepcion on first. The score was tied in the seventh inning. Ray Knight hit a ball past the drawn-in Tim Foli that struck Foster and kept on rolling. In the meantime, the Red runners kept on running. Legally.

Who's on Third?

82

Since there was no force play in effect, the runner from second has sole right to the base, as he arrived there first. The other two are trespassers, and are out.

Babe Herman of the 1926 Dodgers "tripled" into a double play under similar circumstances. Herman, who, in his younger years, ran the bases like a runaway stagecoach, became much too cautious after that double-play incident. Teammates were constantly complaining about him, because they were passing the hesitant Herman on the base paths. He never

wanted to end up on the
same base with a teammate again!
Since that day, when someone says, "The
Dodgers have three men on base," a listener with a keen
sense of humor will ask, "Which base?"

The Unkindest Touch

Yes, the runner should have retouched second after the catch. Then,
with the ball dead, he could have advanced. The award of two
bases would have been made from his original base. Rule 7.05 [i].

A Risky Play

No. Since the batter-runner advanced at least one base, the
obstruction is waived off. The other advanced past third at
his own risk, and his out stands. Rule 6.08 [c].

CATCHING

The Karate Chop

Back when Randy Hundley was the catcher for the Cubs, and Gene Mauch was the manager of the Expos, there was no specific rule that covered a back stop's right to enter a dugout to catch a pop fly. Hundley entered the Montreal dugout one day to make what appeared to be a legal catch, but Mauch hit the Bruin backstop with a karate chop, causing the catcher to drop the ball. Was Mauch's act legal?

84

Answer on page 90.

Firm Control of Body

The Dodgers' Brett Butler is on third base with one out when Juan Samuel lifts a high pop foul towards the San Diego dugout. Padre catcher

Benito Santiago drifts toward
the dugout, and when he sees that the ball is
fading farther toward him than he had thought, he steps
into the dugout to make the catch. Should he have permitted
the ball to fall to the ground untouched?

Answer on page 91.

Suicide Squeeze

85

In the bottom of the ninth inning, Shawon Dunston of the Cubs,
who is at third base, represents the winning run. Mark Grace is the
batter with one out. Grace is interfered with by the catcher as he attempts a
suicide squeeze bunt on the first pitch to him. Dunston, who is running on
the pitch, is an easy out at the plate when the catcher picks up the ball in
fair territory and applies the tag. Does Grace get first base on the
catcher's interference? Is Dunston out?

Answer on page 92.

Clean Catch?

The Houston Astros have Jeff Bagwell on second base, Craig Biggio on first, and Ken Caminiti at the plate with a three-two count and two out. Caminiti swings and misses the pay-off pitch, which bounces off the catcher's glove and becomes pinned to the chest protector of the Braves backstop. Can all the runners advance? Or is it a legal catch?

Answer on page 92.

86

Fan Interference

The catcher, in chasing a foul pop fly, brakes to a halt near the dugout seats. A fan clearly leans over the rail, onto the field, and interferes with the flight of the ball. The catcher fails to make the catch. Does the batter get another chance?

Answer on page 92–93.

A Catchy
Situation

In Game 3 of the 1975 World Series, the Reds and Red Sox are tied 1-1 in the bottom half of the ninth inning. They are also tied at one game apiece.

Cesar Geronimo leads off the Reds' inning with a bloop single. Then the next batter drops down a bunt directly in front of the plate. But he is slow to move out of the batters' box. Red Sox catcher Carlton Fisk has to shove the batter out of the way with his glove and pick the ball up with his bare hand. Fisk's throw beats Geronimo by plenty of time at second; but because of the bodily contact at the plate, his off-balance throw goes into center field. Geronimo continues to third.

The Red Sox want the batter to be called out for interference. In fact, they want two outs, for that's what they would have gotten if Fisk's throw had been on the mark. What do they get?

Answer on page 93.

Throwing
Behind the Runner

Trick plays can, indeed, be "tricky." Take the catcher's pickup move for example.

A Mariner catcher was trying to contain the Royals' base runner, who was on first base. What the catcher decided to do was to look at the pitcher, as if throwing to him, but to throw to first base instead. The first time he attempted this trick move, his first baseman was daydreaming. The catcher's throw sailed past the unsuspecting first baseman and rolled into the right-field corner while the runner scored. How could the catcher have prevented this unfortunate set of circumstances from taking place?

Answer on page 94.

BASEBALL QUOTABLE

Hall-of-Famer Yogi Berra once said, "So what if I'm ugly? I never saw anyone hit with his face."

Colorful Quotes

1. What American League pitcher said of his first trip to Yankee Stadium, "The first time I ever came into a game there, I got in the bullpen car, and they told me to lock the doors"?

2. This pitcher apparently got tired of being asked trite questions by reporters. Once, after surrendering a home run that cost him a 1–0 defeat, he was asked what it was he had thrown to game hero Tony Conigliaro. The succinct reply was, "It was a baseball."

3. This manager did so well, Cardinals owner August Busch, who was eighty-five at the time, told him he could have a lifetime contract. The St. Louis skipper countered with, "Whose lifetime? Yours or mine?"

4. This colorful character was a fine pitcher. His World Series ledger was golden: 6–0 with a 2.86 ERA. When asked to explain his success, he attributed it to "clean living and a fast outfield."

a. Glenn Wilson
b. Casey Stengel

c. Deion Sanders
d. Yogi Berra

Answer on page 95.

89

CATCHING ANSWERS

The Karate Chop

Yes, at the time it was. It was considered to be no different than an outfielder reaching into the stands to catch a ball and being hit with a karate chop by an overzealous fan. Both acts would definitely be placed under the category of unethical and unsportsmanlike conduct, but at the same time, they would also be classified as legal plays.

Today, a fielder or catcher may reach or step into, or go into, the dugout with one or both feet to make a catch, and if he holds the ball, the catch shall be allowed. The ball is in play. Rule 7.04 [c].

90

Firm Control of Body

No. Santiago made a good play. He can make a legal throw from the dugout or he can step out of the dugout to make a play.

Now, suppose that, after he had made the catch, he slipped and fell to the dugout floor? That would have been a bad play. The player has to maintain firm control of his body in order to make a follow-up play. If he loses control of his body, the ball becomes dead and all runners advance one base. Thus in the above example, Butler would score and the Dodgers would win the game. Rule 7.04 [c].

In 1947 big Ernie Lombardi was winding down his Hall-of-Fame career with the New York Giants. One day at the Polo Grounds, in a game with the Giants, St. Louis had Enos Slaughter on third base when Al Schoendienst lifted a foul pop toward the Redbirds' bench. Lombardi went into the dugout to make the catch but subsequently slipped and fell, and Slaughter was waved home by the plate umpire.

Suicide Squeeze

Grace is awarded first base and Dunston scores, if the Cubs manager elects the penalty over the play. Whenever the catcher interferes with the batter, the offensive player is awarded first base. If, on such interference, a runner is attempting to score on a squeeze or steal from third, the ball is proclaimed dead and the runner on third scores.

Clean Catch?

The catch is legal. Caminiti is out on a strikeout and the Astros are retired on outs. Rule 6.05 [b].

Fan Interference

The batter does not get another chance to hit when a fan interferes with a player attempting to make a catch on the playing field. If the player is leaning

across the rail into the stands,
the fan has a right to the ball. In the case
illustrated here, however, the batter is out.

Del Rice of the Braves had that happen to him in a
game in Philadelphia. The umpire called the batter out because
Rice was standing and reaching for the ball on the playing field, and he
could have caught it if the fan had not interfered.

A Catchy Situation

93

Nothing. The plate umpire disallows the appeal, claiming that the
contact was accidental, not purposeful. Joe Morgan, the next batter,
singles, Geronimo scores, and the game is over.

That play may have cost the Red Sox the 1975 World Series.
The Reds went on to win the Series in seven games. Had the call
gone the other way, the Red Sox might have won Game 3.
If they had, they could have won the World Series in
six games.

Throwing Behind the Runner

He should have informed his first baseman in advance, thus avoiding the disastrous consequences.

Choo-Choo Coleman, catcher for the 1962 Mets, tried to hold the Dodgers' speedster Maury Wills close by using that play. Coleman actually executed the play well. The throw was hard and accurate. There was only one problem: the Mets had a first baseman by the name of Marv Throneberry.

The "Marvelous One" was daydreaming, and he caught the throw right on his forehead. The ball glanced off his head and rolled between the right and center fielders. Wills laughed all the way 'round the bases. The moral is, the catcher can look the wrong way, but the first baseman can't.

94

ANSWERS

"Who Said It?" Match-ups

Page 24	Page 25	Page 35
Managers' Quotes	**Humor**	**More Managers**

Page 24		Page 25		Page 35	
1. b	4. d	1. c	4. e	1. d	3. a
2. a	5. f	2. d	5. a	2. c	4. b
3. c	6. e	3. b			

Page 59	Page 77	Page 89
Managers, Last Call	**More Humor**	**Colorful Quotes**

Page 59		Page 77		Page 89	
1. d	4. c	1. a	4. e	1. b	3. d
2. e	5. a	2. c	5. b	2. a	4. c
3. b		3. d			

ABOUT THE AUTHORS

Dom Forker has studied the National Pastime closely since the age of six, when he adopted the legendary Joe DiMaggio as his diamond hero. Coincidentally, DiMaggio, playing in his first World Series, got three hits on the day that the author was born. A player, coach, and umpire on the college, high school, sandlot, and Little League levels, he is an authority on the baseball rule book. Dom Forker is married and has three sons, all of whom, like their father, are avid baseball fans.

Wayne Stewart was born and raised in Donora, Pennsylvania, a town that has produced several big-league baseball players including Stan Musial and the father-son Griffeys. Covering the baseball world as a writer for over 25 years, he has interviewed such players as Nolan Ryan, Bob Gibson, Warren Spahn, and Willie Stargell, and produced nearly 600 articles for such national publications as *Baseball Digest* and *Boy's Life*. Wayne Stewart is married and has two sons.